Francesca Moody Productions

FEELING AFRAID AS IF SOMETHING TERRIBLE IS GOING TO HAPPEN

by Marcelo Dos Santos

Feeling Afraid As If Something Terrible Is Going To Happen premiered in Roundabout at Summerhall as part of the Edinburgh Fringe Festival in 2022, after which it transferred to the Bush Theatre, London, in November 2023.

FEELING AFRAID AS IF SOMETHING TERRIBLE IS GOING TO HAPPEN

by Marcelo Dos Santos

CREATIVE TEAM

Writer	Marcelo Dos Santos
Director	Matthew Xia
Set & Costume Designer	Kat Heath
Lighting Designer	Elliot Griggs
Sound Designer	Max Pappenheim
Stage Manager	Chloë Forestier-Walker
Associate Director	Blythe Stewart
Additional Dramaturgical Support	Oscar Toeman
Production Manager	Jack Boissieux

CAST

THE COMEDIAN　　　　　　　　　　Samuel Barnett

PRODUCERS

Francesca Moody Productions
Bush Theatre
Kater Gordon (Co-Producer)
Dianne Roberts (Associate Producer)

PRESS AND MARKETING for FRANCESCA MOODY PRODUCTIONS

PR	About Grace
Marketing Consultant	Bonnie Royal

EDINBURGH 2022

Producer	Harriet Bolwell
Production Manager	Ed Borgnis
PR	SM Publicity

Special thanks to Ariel Levy, Artistic Solutions, Atlas Couriers, Bush Theatre, Centreline Fabrications, Dianne Roberts, DMLK, Giles Moody, Julie Clare, Matthew Littleford, Mcdougalls, Michael Windsor Ungureanu, National Theatre, Paines Plough, Richard Lakos, Riverside Studios, Simon Blakey, Theodora Alexander, Waterperry Opera Festival and White Light.

BIOGRAPHIES

MARCELO DOS SANTOS | Writer
Marcelo is an award-winning Latinx British-Brazilian-Australian writer.

He has been a writer on attachment at the National Theatre, the Bush Theatre, HighTide Festival Theatre as well as the Royal Court Theatre. Marcelo was also a member of the BBC Drama Room and is developing several television projects with companies including Avalon TV, Mam Tor Productions and Drama Republic.

In 2014 he adapted the critically acclaimed best-selling Zizou Corder novel *Lionboy* for Complicité which toured extensively in the UK (★★★★ *Guardian*, *Mail on Sunday*, *The Times*, *Evening Standard*, *Financial Times*) and internationally, including to the New Victory Theater on Broadway where it was Critics Choice in the *New York Times*.

In 2022, Marcelo won a Scotsman Fringe First award for Excellence in New Writing for his monologue *Feeling Afraid As If Something Terrible Is Going To Happen* directed by Matthew Xia, starring Tony and Olivier-nominated Samuel Barnett (*The History Boys*, *Dirk Gently's Holistic Detective Agency*) produced by Francesca Moody, producer of Phoebe Waller-Bridge's *Fleabag* and Richard Gadd's *Baby Reindeer*.

Critics hailed the play as: 'a masterclass in comic delivery' (★★★★★ WhatsOnStage), 'razor sharp' (*Scotsman*) and 'Frank, funny and occasionally filthy… following in the footsteps of *Fleabag*' (*The Independent*).

Backstairs Billy recently marked Marcelo's West End debut as a writer, and starred Luke Evans and Penelope Wilton in the lead roles. The show was directed by Michael Grandage and produced by MGC Productions.

Previous theatre work includes *Trigger Warning* (Camden People's Theatre); *The End of History* (a site-responsive play staged at St Giles In The Fields in Soho); *Open Plan* (Royal Welsh College of Music and Drama); *Knights* (directed by Michael Longhurst, Tristan Bates Theatre); *New Labour* (directed by Richard Wilson, RADA) and *Play Without a Title* (a new interpretation of Lorca's final unfinished play for Oxford School of Drama).

MATTHEW XIA | Director
Matthew Xia is the award-winning Artistic Director of ATC (Actors Touring Company). He was previously Associate Artistic Director at the Royal Exchange Theatre, Manchester; Director-in-Residence at The Liverpool Everyman & Playhouse; and Associate Director at Theatre Royal Stratford East. He was an Associate Artist at the Nottingham Playhouse alongside James Graham and Amanda Whittington from 2018–2022.

Matthew has directed some of the UK's most talented actors, including Daniel Kaluuya, Cynthia Erivo, Maxine Peake, David Haig, Karl Collins, Samuel Barnett, Malachi Kirby, David Moorst, Erin Doherty and Joseph Quinn.

Directing includes *Tambo & Bones* (ATC/Stratford East); the Olivier Award-winning *Hey Duggee – The Live Theatre Show* (Kenny Wax Family Entertainment/Cuffe & Taylor); the Fringe First award-winning *Feeling Afraid As If Something Terrible Is Going To Happen* (FMP/Roundabout); *The Architect* (GDIF/ATC/SLDF); *RICE* (ATC/Orange Tree); *The Wiz* (Ameena Hamid Productions/Hope Mill/BBC Big Night of Musicals); *Family Tree* (GDIF/ATC/Belgrade/Brixton House); *846 LIVE* (Theatre Royal Stratford East/GDIF); *Amsterdam* (ATC/Orange Tree/Plymouth Theatre Royal); *Blood Knot* (Orange Tree); *Eden* (Hampstead Theatre); *One Night In Miami…* (Nottingham Playhouse/Bristol Old Vic/HOME); *Into the Woods* and *Frankenstein* (Royal Exchange Theatre); *Wish List* (Royal Exchange Theatre/Royal Court); *Shebeen* (Nottingham Playhouse/Theatre Royal Stratford East); *Sleeping Beauty* (Theatre Royal Stratford East); *Dublin Carol* (Sherman Theatre); *Blue/Orange* and *The Sound of Yellow* (Young Vic); *Sizwe Banzi Is Dead* (Genesis Future Director Award Winner – Young Vic/Eclipse); *The Blacks* (Co-Director, Theatre Royal Stratford East); *I Was Looking at the Ceiling and Then I Saw the Sky* (Co-Director, Theatre Royal Stratford East/The Barbican); *Suckerpunch Boom Suite* (The Barbican/NitroBEAT).

Matthew has worked with an array of renowned writers as a director and a dramaturg, including Joe Penhall, Vikki Stone, Arinzé Kene, April D'Angelis, Katherine Soper, David Levi-Addai, Yasmin Joseph, Mojisola Adebayo, and Nessah Murthy. He has been a respected panellist for the Evening Standard Future Fund, Yale Drama Series, the Alfred Fagon Award, BEAM, the Bruntwood Prize and most recently the Eurovision Song Contest!

As DJ Excalibah, Matthew became the first DJ to join BBC 1Xtra with his hip-hop show – aged only 19. He has played most major festivals and clubs in the UK and Europe including Glastonbury, Ministry of Sound, and Fabric. Excalibah performed for a global audience of over 3 billion as a headline DJ at the London 2012 Paralympic Opening Ceremony.

Composing/sound design includes *The People Are Singing* (Royal Exchange); *Free Run* (Underbelly); *That's The Way To Do It* (TimeWontWait); *Pass the Baton* and *Bolero Remixed* (New London Orchestra); *Da Boyz*, *Family Man*, *The Snow Queen*, *Hansel & Gretel*, *Medea*, and *Squid* (Theatre Royal Stratford East).

Matthew is a founding member of Act for Change and Vice Chair at Cardboard Citizens. In 2019, he was awarded an Honorary Doctorate from the University of the Arts London for his efforts to make theatre universally accessible by working to promote minority groups as theatre leaders, makers and consumers.

SAMUEL BARNETT | The Comedian

Samuel is an Olivier and two-time Tony nominated actor. He will revive his role in the London transfer of *Feeling Afraid As If Something Terrible Is Going To Happen* at the Bush Theatre. This one man play, written by Marcelo Dos Santos was a critically acclaimed and award-winning hit at the 2022 Edinburgh Fringe Festival.

In 2022 Samuel starred opposite Ralph Fiennes in *Straight Line Crazy*, directed by Nicholas Hytner at the Bridge Theatre. On screen he filmed the role of Cecil Beaton in the feature film *Lee*, opposite Kate Winslet due for release this December. Sam will also star in upcoming comedy film *And Mrs* alongside Harriet Walter and Aisling Bea.

In 2016 Samuel starred in the title role of *Dirk Gently's Holistic Detective Agency* for BBC America opposite Elijah Wood. The show, created by Max Landis, was inspired by the novel of the same name by Douglas Adams and ran for two seasons.

Samuel received his second Tony nomination in 2014 for his portrayal of Viola in *Twelfth Night* on Broadway, directed by Tim Carroll. His first Tony nomination was for the original production of Alan Bennett's acclaimed *History Boys*, for which he also won the Drama Desk Award and was nominated for an Olivier Award. In 2006 he was nominated for Most Promising Newcomer at the British Independent Film Awards for the film adaptation.

Other screen credits include *The Lady in the Van*, *Jupiter Ascending*, *The Amazing Mr Blunden* (Sky); *Penny Dreadful* (Showtime); *Twenty Twelve* and *Beautiful People* (BBC).

KAT HEATH | Set & Costume Designer

Kat Heath trained in Design for Performance at Wimbledon School of Art and Central Saint Martins, London.

Recent set and costume designs include *Dixon and Daughters* (National Theatre); *New Electric Ballroom* (Gate, Dublin); *The Third Day: Autumn* and *Audiences of the Future* (for Punchdrunk and HBO/Sky); *Typical Girls* (Sheffield Crucible); *The Bar at the Edge of Time*, *Fire Songs*, *Sensory Studio*, *The Isle of Brimsker*, *2065* and *A Night Out in Nature* (all for Frozen Light); *A Curious Quest*, *Route 158* and *Woolwich Hall of Fame* (Punchdrunk Enrichment); *The Nutcracker* (Moxie Brawl at Cambridge Junction); *Through This Mist* (Clean Break Courtyard); *Our Man in Havana* (Watermill Theatre); *Odds On* (Dante or Die); *Il Tabarro* (Copenhagen Opera Festival); *Peaky Blinders* (Rambert); *Punk Alley* (Southbank Centre); *MSND* (Rift); *The Forest of Forgotten Discos* (Contact Theatre); *The Redux Project* (Richard Dedomenici at Battersea Arts Centre and for BBC); *The Hollow Hotel* (DifferencEngine); *Macbeth*, *I'm Super Thanks* (Proteus); *The Burning Tower*, *Bush Bazaar* and *Fun Palaces* (Bush); *Bridges y Puentes* (Theatre Royal Stratford East); *You've Changed* and *Big Girl's Blouse* (TransCreative); *Così fan tutte* (Bury Court Opera); *The Importance of Being Earnest* and *The Two Worlds of Charlie F* (Theatre Royal Haymarket); *L'Orfeo*, *La Bohème* and *Dido and Aeneas* (Silent Opera); and *Girls in Peacetime Want to Dance* (Belle & Sebastian).

ELLIOT GRIGGS | Lighting Designer

Theatre work includes *Blue Mist, all of it, Purple Snowflakes and Titty Wanks, A Fight Against, On Bear Ridge* and *Yen* (Royal Court); *Beautiful Thing* (Theatre Royal Stratford East/Leeds Playhouse); *Jitney* (Old Vic/Leeds Playhouse/Headlong); *Amélie the Musical* (Criterion Theatre/The Other Palace/Watermill Theatre/UK tour); *The Wild Duck* (Almeida); *The Lover/The Collection* (Harold Pinter Theatre); *Fleabag* (Wyndham's Theatre/New York/Soho Theatre/Edinburgh Festival/tour); *No Pay? No Way!, Queens of the Coal Age* and *The Night Watch* (Royal Exchange); *Sleepova, The P Word* and *Hir* (Bush Theatre); *An Octoroon* and *Pomona* (National Theatre/Orange Tree); *Ivan and the Dogs* (Young Vic); *Richard III* (Headlong); *Disco Pigs* (Trafalgar Studios/Irish Rep, NY); *The Swell, The Misfortune of the English, Last Easter, The Sugar Syndrome, Low Level Panic, Sheppey* and *buckets* (Orange Tree); *The Oracles* (Punchdrunk).

Awards include Off West End Award for Best Lighting Designer (*Pomona*).

MAX PAPPENHEIM | Sound Designer

Recent theatre includes *Boy Out The City, The Night of the Iguana* and *Cruise* (West End); *A Doll's House Part 2* and *The Way of the World* (Donmar Warehouse); *Henry V* (Shakespeare's Globe/Headlong); *Anthology, Blackout Songs, Sea Creatures, Linck and Mülhahn, The Fever Syndrome* and *Labyrinth* (Hampstead Theatre); *The Children* (Royal Court/Broadway); *Old Bridge* (Bush Theatre. Off West End Award for Sound Design, Olivier Award for Outstanding Achievement in an Affiliate Theatre); *Ophelias Zimmer* (Royal Court/Schaubühne); *Village Idiot* and *One Night in Miami* (Nottingham Playhouse); *The Ridiculous Darkness* (Gate Theatre); *Humble Boy, Blue/Heart* and *The Distance* (Orange Tree Theatre); *The Cherry Orchard* and *A Kettle of Fish* (Yard Theatre); *The Mirror Crack'd, Wish You Were Dead, Being Mr Wickham, The Habit of Art, The Homecoming* and *My Cousin Rachel* (UK tours).

Opera and ballet includes *The Limit* (Royal Ballet); *The Marriage of Figaro* (Salzburger Festspiele); *Miranda* (Opéra Comique, Paris); *Hansel and Gretel* (BYO/Opera Holland Park); *Scraww* (Trebah Gardens); *Carmen: Remastered* (ROH/Barbican).

BLYTHE STEWART | Associate Director

Blythe has worked as an associate and director for a range of companies including the National Theatre, Donmar Warehouse, House Productions, Soho Theatre, and HighTide Festival, as well as drama schools including LAMDA, ArtsEd, Guildhall and Oxford School Of Drama. She has been nominated twice for Best Director at the Off West End Awards.

Recent credits include Associate Director on *The Crucible* (National Theatre/Gielgud Theatre) and Resident Director on *The Curious Incident of the Dog in the Night-Time* (UK and Ireland tour). She was the Donmar Resident Assistant Director between 2019–2020.

JACK BOISSIEUX | Production Manager
Training: Royal Central School of Speech and Drama.

Credits include *The Choir of Man* and *Bluey's Big Play* (international); Festival Production Manager (Waterperry Opera Festival 2021–2023); *Pied Piper* (Battersea Arts Centre/national tour); *The Borrowers* (Theatre by the Lake); *An Improbable Musical* (Hackney Empire/national tour); *Berlusconi* (Southwark Playhouse Elephant); *Saving Face* (Curve); National Youth Theatre Annual Fundraising Gala (2021–2023); *Lay Down Your Burdens* (Barbican/national tour); *Punchdrunk Enrichment* (multiple venues); *Habibti Driver* (Octagon Theatre); *Anything Is Possible If You Think About It Hard Enough* (Southwark Playhouse); *LAVA* (UK tour); *When We Dead Awaken* (Coronet Theatre); *Jungle Rumble* (Fortune Theatre).

CHLOË FORESTIER-WALKER | Stage Manager
Chloë's stage management work includes *Guys & Dolls*, *A Christmas Carol* and *Straight Line Crazy* (Bridge Theatre); *Feeling Afraid As If Something Terrible Is Going To Happen* (Paines Plough Roundabout, Summerhall); Platinum Jubilee Pageant, *Peggy for You* and *little scratch* (Hampstead Theatre); *Deciphering* (Curious Directive/New Diorama Theatre); *Arthur/Merlin* (Iris Theatre).

KATER GORDON | Co-Producer
Kater is an Emmy Award-winning writer (*Mad Men*) and an Olivier and Tony Award-nominated producer.

Recent projects include *Vanya* (Duke of York's); *2:22 A Ghost Story* (Noël Coward Theatre, Gielgud Theatre, Criterion Theatre, Lyric Theatre, Apollo Theatre, Ahmanson Theatre, Her Majesty's Theatre Melbourne, UK tour); Broadway's *A Doll's House* (Hudson Theatre); *Lemons, Lemons, Lemons, Lemons, Lemons* (Harold Pinter Theatre); Disney's *Newsies* (Troubadour Wembley Theatre); *One Woman Show* (Greenwich House Theatre), and *Kathy and Stella Solve A Murder* (Roundabout, Underbelly, Bristol Old Vic, Manchester HOME).

DIANNE ROBERTS | Associate Producer
Dianne is thrilled to be involved with *Feeling Afraid As If Something Terrible Is Going To Happen* which captivated her at Edinburgh Fringe. She is a producer and investor in an exciting range of productions. She was a producer on Olivier and Tony award-winning *Girl from the North Country* and more recently, Disney's *Newsies*. Other recent shows include *2:22 A Ghost Story*, *Vanya* and *Patriots*. Her support for new productions include several Edinburgh fringe shows and working with a new company creating original musical theatre. Her philanthropic work includes support for the Musical Theatre and Jazz programmes at the Royal Academy of Music.

Francesca Moody Productions

Francesca Moody Productions commissions, develops and presents brave, entertaining and compelling new theatre. They work with the UK's leading playwrights and discover and nurture new talent to produce bold, award-winning shows with universal appeal and commercial potential.

Since launching in 2018 the company has been awarded an Olivier and four Scotsman Fringe Firsts, been nominated for a Tony Award, and produced work in London, New York, on tour across the UK and at the Edinburgh Festival.

Productions include: *Kathy and Stella Solve a Murder* (Underbelly Edinburgh, Bristol Old Vic, HOME Manchester, Roundabout), *Feeling Afraid As If Something Terrible Is Going To Happen* (Bush Theatre, Roundabout), *Nutcracker* (Southbank Centre), *Never Have I Ever* (Chichester Festival Theatre), *School Girls; Or, The African Mean Girls Play* (Lyric Hammersmith), *An Oak Tree* (Festival d'Avignon, Royal Lyceum Theatre Edinburgh), *A Doll's House* (Hudson Theatre, New York), *A Streetcar Named Desire* (Phoenix Theatre), *Lemons Lemons Lemons Lemons Lemons* (Harold Pinter Theatre), *Berlusconi: A New Musical* (Southwark Playhouse Elephant), *Mum* (Soho Theatre), *Leopards* (Rose Theatre) and *Baby Reindeer* (Bush Theatre, Roundabout).

FMP are also the creators of Shedinburgh Fringe Festival, an online live-streamed festival of theatre, comedy and music created in lieu of the Edinburgh Fringe in 2020. Since its launch the festival has raised over £40,000 towards a fund to support the next generation of artists to make it to the Fringe.

FMP is led by Francesca Moody MBE who is best known as the original producer of the multi-award-winning *Fleabag* by Phoebe Waller-Bridge, which she has produced globally on behalf on DryWrite, most recently at the Wyndhams Theatre, when it was also recorded and broadcast by NT Live, playing in cinemas throughout the world. In 2020 Francesca led and coordinated the Fleabag for Charity campaign and later the Theatre Community Fund with Phoebe Waller-Bridge and Olivia Colman, raising over £2million to support theatrical artists and professionals whose livelihoods and creative futures have been threatened in the wake of Covid-19.

FRANCESCA MOODY PRODUCTIONS

Executive Producer	**Francesca Moody**
Associate Producer	**Grace Dickson**
Production Assistant	**Elly Roberts**
Finance Manager	**Charlotte Walton**

Twitter: @FMP_Theatre
Instagram: @francesca_moody_productions
Facebook: facebook.com/FMoodyProductions
Email: hello@francescamoody.com
www.francescamoody.com

Bush Theatre

We make theatre for London. Now.

Opened in 1972, the Bush is a world-famous home for new plays and an internationally renowned champion of playwrights. We discover, nurture and produce the best new writers from the widest range of backgrounds from our home in a distinctive corner of west London.

The Bush has won over 100 awards and developed an enviable reputation for its acclaimed productions nationally and internationally. We are excited by exceptional new voices, stories and perspectives – particularly those with contemporary bite which reflect the vibrancy of British culture now.

Located in the renovated old library on Uxbridge Road in the heart of Shepherd's Bush, the Bush continues to create a space where all communities can be part of its future and call the theatre home.

bushtheatre.co.uk

Bush Theatre

Artistic Director	Lynette Linton
Executive Director	Mimi Findlay
Associate Artistic Director	Daniel Bailey
Development & Marketing Assistant	Nicima Abdi
Development Officer	Laura Aiton
Senior Marketing Manager	Shannon Clarke
Head of Development	Jocelyn Cox
Associate Dramaturg	Titilola Dawudu
Finance Assistant	Lauren Francis
Young Company Director	Katie Greenall
Technical & Buildings Manager	Jamie Haigh
Head of Finance	Neil Harris
Marketing Officer	Laela Henley-Rowe
Associate Producer	Nikita Karia
Community Assistant & Theatre Administrator	Joanne Leung
PA to the Executive	April Miller
Development Officer	Eilidh Nurse
Senior Producer	Oscar Owen
Event Sales Manager & Technician	Charlie Sadler
Venue Manager (Theatre)	Ade Seriki
Press Manager	Martin Shippen
Community Producer	Holly Smith
Marketing Manager	Ed Theakston
Venue Manager (Bar)	Adaeze Uyanwah
General Manager	Angela Wachner
Assistant Venue Manager (Box Office)	Robin Wilks

DUTY MANAGERS
Sara Dawood, Molly Elson, Rae Harm, Nick Malkewitz,
Madeleine Simpson-Kent, Laetitia Some & Anna-May Wood.

VENUE SUPERVISORS
Antony Baker, Addy Caulder-James, Judd Launder & Coral Richards.

VENUE ASSISTANTS
Caitlyn Allen, Louise Barclay Johnson, Maryse Baya, Will Byam-Shaw,
Nikki Farrell, Kane Feagan, Lydia Feerick, Matias Hailu, Anastasiya Hamolka,
Kika Hendry, Bo Leandro, Nzuzi Malemda, Carys Murray, Louis Nicholson,
Jennifer Okolo, Kyra Palma, Kathrine Payne, Saroja-Lily Ratnavel,
Merle Wheldon-Posner & Nefertari Williams.

BOARD OF TRUSTEES
Uzma Hasan (Chair), Kim Evans, Keerthi Kollimada, Lynette Linton,
Anthony Marraccino, Jim Marshall, Rajiv Nathwani, Stephen Pidcock,
Catherine Score & Cllr Mercy Umeh.

Bush Theatre, 7 Uxbridge Road, London W12 8LJ
Box Office: 020 8743 5050 | Administration: 020 8743 3584
Email: info@bushtheatre.co.uk | bushtheatre.co.uk

Alternative Theatre Company Ltd
The Bush Theatre is a Registered Charity
and a company limited by guarantee.
Registered in England no. 1221968 Charity no. 270080

THANK YOU

The Bush Theatre would like to thank all its supporters whose valuable contributions have helped us to create a platform for our future and to promote the highest quality new writing, develop the next generation of creative talent, lead innovative community engagement work and champion diversity.

MAJOR DONORS
Charles Holloway
Jim & Michelle Gibson
Georgia Oetker
Tim & Cathy Score
Susie Simkins
Jack Thorne

SHOOTING STARS
Jim & Michelle Gibson

LONE STARS
Jax & Julian Bull
Clyde Cooper
Charles Holloway
Anthony Marraccino & Mariela Manso
Jim Marshall
Georgia Oetker
Susie Simkins

HANDFUL OF STARS
Charlie Bigham
Judy Bollinger
Sue Fletcher
Simon & Katherine Johnson
Joanna Kennedy
Garry Lawrence
Vivienne Lukey
Aditya Mittal
Sam & Jim Murgatroyd
Martha Plimpton
Bhagat Sharma
Dame Emma Thompson

RISING STARS
Martin Blackburn
David Brooks
Catharine Browne
Lauren Clancy
Tim Clark
Richard & Sarah Clarke
Susan Cuff
Matthew Cushen
Ivo Detelinov
Preslava Detelinov
Jubilee Easo
Kim Evans
Mimi Findlay
Jack Gordon
Hugh & Sarah Grootenhuis
Thea Guest
Sarah Harrison
Uzma Hasan
Lesley Hill & Russ Shaw
Melanie Johnson
Ann Joseph
Davina & Malcolm Judelson
Mike Lewis
Lynette Linton
Michael McCoy
Judy Mellor
Caro Millington
Kate Pakenham
Mark & Anne Paterson
Stephen Pidcock
Miguel & Valeri Ramos Handal
Karen & John Seal
James St. Ville KC
Oliver Stocken
Peter Tausig
Joe Tinston & Amelia Knott
Jan Topham

CORPORATE SPONSORS
Biznography
Casting Pictures Ltd.
Nick Hern Books
S&P Global
The Agency
Wychwood Media

TRUSTS & FOUNDATIONS
Backstage Trust
Buffini Chao Foundation
Christina Smith Foundation
Daisy Trust
Esmée Fairbairn Foundation
The Foyle Foundation
Garfield Weston Foundation
Garrick Charitable Trust
Hammersmith United Charities
The Harold Hyam Wingate Foundation
Jerwood Arts
John Lyon's Charity
Martin Bowley Charitable Trust
The Thistle Trust
The Weinstock Fund

And all the donors who wish to remain anonymous.

 Supported by **ARTS COUNCIL ENGLAND**

If you are interested in finding out how to be involved, please visit **bushtheatre.co.uk/support-us** email **development@bushtheatre.co.uk** or call **020 8743 3584**.

FEELING AFRAID AS IF SOMETHING TERRIBLE IS GOING TO HAPPEN

Marcelo Dos Santos

Acknowledgements

Thanks to Gabby Vautier (ImPOSSIBLE Producing), Emma Cameron, Emily Hamilton, Zbigniew Kotkiewicz, Jane Fallowfield, Oscar Toeman, the Royal Court and Arts Council England for their support on the initial workshop; Simon Blakey and Seán Butler at The Agency; Maddie Hindes, Sarah Liisa Wilkinson, Deborah Halsey, Matt Applewhite, Tamara von Werthern, Jon Barton, Robin Booth, Ian Higham, Tim Digby-Bell, Beth Fisher, Sarah Lambie, Marcus O'Neill, Isabelle Culkin and Nick Hern at Nick Hern Books; Kenny Emson, Jamie Hakim and Patrick Welch for the chats.

M.D.S.

*To Rhys Warrington,
for changing everything*

This text went to press before the end of rehearsals and so may differ slightly from the play as performed.

A MAN. *A microphone. A microphone stand and stool.*

I'm thirty-six, which is fine.
It's fine.
Is it? I mean it's technically allowed, so.
I'm thirty-six and up until very recently, I'd never been in a proper relationship.
Which is also fine because I have absolutely no fear of dying alone.
Because I'm a very chilled, in-the-moment, sexually adventurous sort of human person.
For example a gentleman once asked if he could eat sushi off me and seeing as it was a Tuesday and life has no meaning I said: 'yeah'.
You know how you do: like, 'yeah'.
Lower-case, super-cool; 'yeah'.
Like you're so tired at the thought of being a human sushi platter AGAIN that you can't even bring yourself to capitalise the y.
What was a little cheeky was that he told me to bring my own sushi.
He offered to pay me back though so romance not entirely dead.
It might have died later though when it turned out the supermarket sashimi had curdled on the bus ride over.

Beat.

Sorry.

Beat.

I'll start again.

I'm thirty-six, and I'm a comedian, although I prefer the title 'sad for pay'.
Or 'professional neurotic'.
Or 'a bit like, oh you know what's-his-name with the hair, but not as funny'.

Sorry.

I'm thirty-six, I'm a comedian and I'm about to kill my boyfriend.

/

He has excellent teeth; very white with a well-judged gum-to-tooth ratio.
He wears long-sleeved, light-blue Oxford shirts and baseball caps, which he is able to take off whenever he wants because his hair is MAGIC.
He's American which explains the cap, the teeth and the fact he didn't immediately smash his phone when we matched.
I've discovered over the years that my accent has currency with Americans, and my man-boy physique holds a strange allure to the formerly fat.
When I first saw him I sent up a silent prayer.
Dear God, please let it be that he used to eat his feelings as a kid, was relentlessly bullied and his parents own a beach house in the Hamptons where we will be wed, amen.

Sorry.
Was the first word I said to him.
Why? He said sounding all American, like they do on the telly.
I don't know but always good to get it in first.
He smiled.
His smile of course, is devastating.
I am devastated.
What's wrong?
Nothing I said. Or is there? Has someone had an accident? Is there an emergency? Do you need to go? Or shall I go, leave you to it? Yeah let's do that. Let me pay for your drink and I'll go.
You're funny? he said, and I chose to think the rising of his voice at the end of the sentence? was his accent rather than a question.

We're sat on wobbly chairs on the pavement outside a Hackney Downs pub drinking gin and tonics.
It's early summer; those two first hot days where everyone flashes their ankles and pretends they live somewhere actually nice.

There are maybe a hundred people strolling the streets, looking lovely and tan, successfully ignoring the fact we're all going to die.
Probably quite soon.
It's always amazing to me that.
Why is no one freaking out more?
Why aren't we already in the bunker?
Why am I the only one in a constant state of panic?
Why are we just doing this? This.
Why aren't we running around screaming?
Why do I have to do all the screaming?
I mean I don't but inside I do.
Inside it is… deafening.

He's looking at me.
Sorry, I have resting sad face, but I'm having a lovely time.
He smiled.
That smile.

We get down to business.
This is, after all, an interview.
We state our biographies at each other with the wry detachment specific to gay men and forensic pathologists.
Distant dad, anxious mothers, dead bodies, blah blah blah.

He's from Boston, Massachusetts.
Do we like that? No.

Beat.

He comes from Sacramento, California, yes!, Sacramento, California: the whole city just one giant tree-lined street.

Total suburbia, close to San Francisco though, he says.

Cool, I say.

Too cool for me, at least when I was young. Too weird as well. I was a nerdy kid. Now it's too expensive. Like insanely expensive.

He studied at Reed in Portland, Oregon.

Cool.

Actually quite problematic, quite divided in terms of race and income inequality but you know, coffee.

Ha! Just that, one, HA, like a lunatic, but he's funny, he's funny!

Now I'm doing a PhD.

Cool.

In US prison reform and when he goes back to the States I'll go with him, sod it.
Or can we have a place here *and* in New York?
Or San Francisco?
Preference for New York.
I'll have to move fast though before he realises.
Before he works out.
Shit, he's finished talking.

Cool. (I keep saying cool.)

Well not if you are the prisoner with HIV, no.

Of course, no, not cool for them at all. (I mean...)

Actually for a lot of people prison is the only place they're going to get healthcare including HIV medication, so...

I don't know what to say to that so I say:

Sooo.

But yeah that's me, that's why I'm over here living the London life.

'London life' isn't a thing but he doesn't know that so I smile, making sure not to reveal my teeth.
Gum recession, gaps, tea stains.

What about you?

Oh I've been here ten years now. Northern but not northern-northern you know? (He doesn't.) Not northern enough for actual northerners, not cool enough for London.

I love your accent.

'Cheers,' I say. (We're all posh to them.)

What else?

Oh you know, lonely childhood, anxious mother, dead dad blah blah blah.

And what do you do?

Lots of ways to play this, none of them guaranteed to work.

Believe it or not, I'm a comedian. Ta-dah.

It's only later, when I know him better, when I'm able to read him better, when I'm able to decipher what's an American pause and what's a silence that I realise this was a silence…

But tell me about you, tell me about the bod.

He looks confused.

The bod, the body, the muscles I can see through your shirt, Mr Muscle, Mr Gym-Going-Man you.

I may or may not have poked his chest and I'm aware of an accusatory edge to my voice but he really enjoys talking about his regime of high-intensity interval training so we do that for exactly… forty-seven minutes.

It's just about exercise, diet, exercise, diet. I mean it always is. You just have to be really in it.

I think about saying I want to be under it but resist.

Sorry, it's boring.

No, not at all.

I used to be fat, he reveals. Like really fat. And really bullied.

I thank God, thank you God and sigh.
And the evening seems to sigh around us.
The waitress finds us adorable.
Or him adorable.
He tips heavily, inappropriately, so perhaps not to be totally trusted but still, cute.
And then we're talking about bad dates.
We trade the usual stories of bad breath and catfishing and there's a frisson to that because that means this.

This is different.
This is a *good* date.

Now the kiss.
Actually no.
Not yet.
The way he licks his lips and teeth before the kiss, like
a toothpaste commercial.
And he does taste delicious.
Fresh but acid from the gin and tonic.
I would very much like to see his penis.
Which I suspect he knows.
That smile again.

Do you want to go see that exhibition next week then?
Presumably we talked about an exhibition.
I have no memory because at one point in the evening he
accidentally-on-purpose lifted up his shirt to reveal what I think
the kids call: semen gutters… and I lost consciousness.

Yes, I'd love that I say and go for another kiss/lunge.
He kindly reciprocates but delicately so as not to wound peels
himself away.
There will be no fucking tonight.
Which is fine.
Which is good.
Which is what we want.
Which is what will make this one different.
Special.
Or I'll never see him again.

On the way home, I buy a giant Haribo bag from the local shop
and as I eat each sweet, I think exercise, diet, exercise, diet.

On the bus Mum rings.
I shouldn't take it because I'm not in the mood but I do.

Well, she says, I'm alright.
I say really?, she says no.
I say oh.
She's lonely; I have no idea what it's like to be a single woman
her age.

I open up 'The App' as she talks.
Very much the usual faces, torsos, sunsets.
I won't name The App because I'm classy but essentially, it's a dating app which encourages sexual connections and mental-health issues.
Mum is talking about Grandma.
I send an ass pic to a surly jock.
Mum is worried about the elections.
I agree to pound a twink's 'boy pussy' whatever that actually is, and then he goes quiet.
I better go I say.
I better go she echoes and then doesn't.
I better go I repeat
Neither of us goes but neither of us is really there.
Are you okay, she asks?
I say of course.
I message Mike and asks if he wants a shag.

And he writes back:

'yeah'

/

Anyone ever cum blood while having sex and feel like you're going to die?
No one?
Me neither.

/

Mike. Mike? Michael. Yeah!
Michael lives in Hampstead.

Michael is a handsome doctor with a lovely, high, bobbing bum who is outrageously not my husband.
We're the same age, same height, same half-smile.
Same star sign too – Scorpio – but crucially neither of us *feel* like Scorpios.
Our dicks look exactly the same, same size, same slight kink to the left.
I look down and lose track of where he ends and I begin.
He's also a DOCTOR, so... you know: buy a hat.

The problem is the only text he responds to is the 'what's up?' text
'What's up?'
Like we're high-school jocks rather than thirty-somethings with weak chins and suspect bowels.

I tell Michael all about the date with the American.
Michael kisses me passionately, deeply and then asks if I want coke.

I don't want it.
I know I don't want it but I say yes.
So he pulls out a bag of coke from his side table and I see a copy of the really quite obscure and clever book I'm currently reading. I think about us being adorable and comparing notes on the unreliable first-person narrator. Instead we talk about all the guys he's shagged in a four-mile radius.
Quite a few we have in common, which is nice.
And it's good.
It's good we can talk about sex.
It's good we can be so open.
It's queer.
It's political.
It's liberating – and the feeling, the feeling what is the feeling? The edge, the sense of creeping something cold is just the, just the, ju-ju-ju-ju-ju
just the coke, he says when we try and have sex again and can't.
It's three a.m.

We stare at the ceiling in silence, not touching and he turns and looks at me.
We shouldn't have done the coke.
I laugh and he laughs back.

Do you like boxing?
I've never watched it.
I've got really into it for some reason, he says. It's very theatrical.
Which is not an enticement, but I say okay.

His arm keeps cramping so he can't hold me and he doesn't like my arm under his neck but we lie side by side, one whole side of our bodies touching and I start to find myself getting into the boxing, enjoying the satisfying simplicity of a contest where both sides know the rules and each knows what the other wants.

Beat.

And then five, four, three, two, one.

Do you mind going home? I've got an early start.

He's that guy.

/

Anyone ever cum blood while having sex and feel like you're going to die?
No one?
Me neither.

/

Now, it could be that he's American, the American.
That's what I think at first.
The way his eyes don't register sometimes.
The way they sort of glaze over when I'm being hilarious.
He's very American in that way.
But he's kind.
He cares.
He knows words.
You know, clever ugly left-wing words.
Hegemony.
Austerity.
Neoliberalism.
But he also says things like:
Self-love.
Self-care.
Self-actualisation.
I stop myself saying 'the only self I'm interested in is self-abuse' with a little Mae West shrug of the shoulders.
I stop myself because when I say things like that he goes silent and his brown eyes go heavy.
It's date two.
Second dates, or recalls as I call them, are tricky.

If I've somehow aced the first date it usually falls apart on the second.
And if it doesn't I make sure it does.
I'm that guy.

Let's find all the pretty boys in the National Portrait Gallery, because let's face it, that's the only way to make it bearable, I say.
(It's a fun game, you should try it.)
I find one I'm very into: Henry Peter Brougham, first Baron Brougham and Vaux, circa 1778.
Clearly a dirty Tory but just enormous big-dick energy.
Tories by the way are my weakness.
I may never have kissed one but I have eaten cum out of their jockstraps.
A young Alfred Lord Tennyson would get it.
Sir John William Alcock (ooh-er missus) rocking a World War One air force uniform
Heroic and naughty.
The American stops at a Henry Lamb self-portrait.
Handsome, I say.
The American doesn't say anything.
Isn't he?
Not as handsome as you, he says.
And it's a line.
It's got to be a line but he doesn't make it a joke, or laugh it off.
He just looks at me with those John Singer Sargent eyes of his and I find myself going – .
And this is true –
A little weak at the knees.
So shall we do this again?, he asks.
Yes, a thousand times yes.

/

I realise I haven't been on The App forever.
Like literally four days.
Five days.
Maybe even a whole week.
This is something of a record so I'm feeling good about myself.

I boldly greet an astonishing torso I wouldn't normally even attempt.
For the uninitiated, if you don't want to show your face on The App, probably because you're over thirty, cheating or closeted, you can put up a picture of your torso, or and this is quite popular, a sunset.
Never a sunrise, read into that what you will.
(You should read into it: death.)
The astonishing torso sends a picture of his face, it's grainy but enough to establish that he has one and a rather fetching dick pic.
Together the images suggest a human male form which seems to be enough for me at that moment.
I send my location.
'Cool. I can come on my run. Haven't got long though.'

The speed of the encounter, the silence, the ambiguity is what's hot/depressing/hot.
Plus he does actually arrive in his running gear, looks to be about twenty-four, and has a tremendous penis, just terrific, first rate.
Would recommend.

(It's only a matter of time before The App has a star-rating option. Just you wait.)

The jogger doesn't want to kiss, of course.
And actually that feels okay.
He lies back on the bed.
I go to work.
He cums.
I don't.
He leaves.
I don't feel shame.
I try not to feel shame.
Because this is what I wanted.
Because I am a very chilled, in-the-moment, sexually adventurous sort of human person.

/

Three dates.
Four dates.

Five dates.
Five dates with the American and we still haven't had sex.
Five dates which is two more than is normal.
Or sane.
That's what Gavin says.
Gavin is an extremely handsome comedian which shouldn't be allowed but it gets him on the telly, a lot.
What exactly is the hurt that you are trying to overcome in your comedy, Gavin? That your razor-sharp cheekbones get snagged in turtlenecks?
Fuck off.
(The backstage repartee at The Bearcat in Twickenham is sparkling.)
I think it's a little excessive says Djosephine, but she genuinely moved in with her girlfriend Ziggy after two dates.
That's not a joke, it's true, although it's also a joke because she does a whole set on it.
I think, you are terrible cynics and it means he's interested. Like actually interested in me as a person.
Why? You're dreadful?
No one likes you.
Has he been to see your show yet?
No.
Good.
That was a terrible set.
You're not funny.
Et cetera.

/

Date six.
I've shaved my pubes to the bone, because every little helps.
And I've douched, just in case.
We haven't discussed who likes what where yet so I have to be prepared for all eventualities.
I don't really have a preference any more; at this point my sexuality would be best described as passive-aggressive.

Are we going to have sex? I demand over yet another really fun dinner.
(I've only eaten a salad so I'm hanging on by a thread.)

Oh right, he says, which could mean ANYTHING.
I like to take things slow, he says which is... nice?
I guess my face does something because he asks:
Is sex like a big thing for you?
No, not at all. At all.
Then what's the rush?
I don't know.
Is that an English thing?
What?
Saying I don't know when you do.
I don't know. I mean. Yes. Or no. I don't know.
What's going on?

Beat.

What if it's bad?
What if he's repelled by my body?
Because the thing is I can handle rejection, honestly.
I'm used to rejection.
It's actually my safe space but as a rule I prefer to get the rejection over with quickly so I can get back to my healthy diet of *Golden Girls* reruns, hate-stalking famous people I used to know and masturbating to Czech twinks being pissed on.

Beat.

What if we're completely incompatible? What if you take one look at me naked and?
Why do you always assume the worst?
I don't!
I mean you absolutely do. Remember your eye thing?
And it takes me a minute.
The brain tumour?
Oh yeah it wasn't a brain tumour.
Because nine times out of ten it's all in your head he says.
As if my head weren't the place I live in.
I look at his chin and I wonder if it's a bit too big actually, too square, like a parody, like someone had drawn it. He's too... perfect.
Are you okay? he asks.
Totally, sorry was I being boring?
No, you just look sad.

That's impossible, I'm having a brilliant time.
It doesn't have to be jokes the whole time, you know?
Talking of which, do you want to come and see my show on
Friday? I'm playing in Bethnal Green which isn't far from you.
The American nods.
He doesn't smile.
He nods.
Serious.
'That'll take the shine off his bliss,' I think.
That's Beckett.
That's not me.
None of this is me.

/

Dad wanted his wake at the Wetherspoons.
Presumably he wanted to die as he lived.
Sad and a little bit racist.

/

The American turns up on his own.
I told him not to.
I said bring a friend.
Implied in that was bring me into your circle of friends and let's all hang out, let's all go to cool parties together or Mexican bars, people go to Mexican bars right? I've seen them, dreadful people at dreadful Mexican bars let's all go to dreadful Mexican bars, eat fajitas and be dreadful, let's have a massive wedding where we invite all our dreadful friends and one of my dreadful friends gets together with one of your dreadful friends and it's really funny but they actually seem to like each other, and soon we're having regular dinner parties together and maybe they get married and have a baby and name it after one of us because they met at our wedding, you actually because you have a better name, but we both get to be honorary guncles and that's quite nice isn't it? That's actually quite special or maybe we want our own? Oh my God are we having a baby? But what would be the best way, surrogacy or adoption? And would we be good parents? You'd be good obviously, you'd be great, which would hopefully make up for me, minimise the damage but at least

we'd have someone to look after us at the end, not that that's
a guarantee, not that the future is compatible with the past on
that front, not that we can look back any more to understand the
future, the future is the science fiction I read as a kid and
stopped reading as an adult because it wasn't grown up but they
knew didn't they? They saw the fracturing, they saw the
cyborgs and the disasters, the plagues and the floods, how can
we bring children into that future? How dare we? Besides my
child won't like me, as if my child would be at my deathbed as
if we won't die alone, as if we don't die all alone anyway.
But funnily enough he didn't seem to pick up on any of that.
He turns up on his own.
He sat not quite in the front row but basically the front row.
Bolt upright – he has excellent posture.
In the half-light, I can see his white teeth.
They're almost ultraviolet.
He's smiling.
He is absolutely smiling.
And he is clapping.
He's a clapper.
Who knew?
He knows when to clap.
He leads the clapping.
The way the laughter seems to crest like a wave into a clap.
He feels the exact point of the crest and he claps or yes.
Yes.
Slaps his thighs.
He slaps his thigh like an eighteenth-century fop highly
appreciative of my abundant wit but he does not laugh.
The fucker doesn't laugh.
And I'm being quite funny.
I won't do it now because you know, pressure, but I had them.
I had them.
I felt it and they felt it.
Which doesn't always happen.
I mean it doesn't normally, not for a whole set.

Anyone ever cum blood while having sex and feel like you're
going to die?

No one?
Me neither.

It's a tricky opening line.
But it's a litmus test.
If I'm relaxed, if I get the rhythm right and the audience laughs we're going to have a good night.
Anyone ever? – sing-song, familiar
Cum blood while having sex? – still light, don't go dark even though it's dark.
Allow a fraction of a beat for the surprise to land.
And feel like you're going to die? – again light, as surprised as us.
No one? – genuinely curious.
Me neither – in on the joke.
Laugh.

A call-and-response.

I make my voice do this.
Laugh.
I combine an expected word with an unexpected one.
Laugh.
I say things in threes.
Laugh laugh laugh.
The inappropriate phallic vol-au-vents at my dad's funeral – surely it feels like we're overcompensating?
The time the guy ate sushi off me – note the alliteration, sweaty, slippy, sashimi.
My mum watching a film called *Snakes on a Plane* and being shocked by the snakes.
Each line spontaneous.
Each line landing exactly as planned.
Each line a line leading to another line.
And finally a satisfying reveal at the end.
Catharsis, ejaculation, laughter.

It's like being a musician, composer, and conductor.

Or is it like being a butcher?
There is something cold and mechanical to it.
If I chop here.

If I fillet there the flesh comes apart from the bone just so.
It's easy.
Like everything is easy when you know how.
Like driving.
But people don't applaud you for driving.
People don't love you for your three-point turn.
Or tattoo your face on their bum for a nifty reverse park.
I guess it's the love that's the difference.
But then drivers don't need the applause.
A butcher is quite relaxed, I assume about what the lamb thinks of him.
Just as well.

But I care, of course, I do.
I'm a comedian.
I'm very obvious, entirely transparent.
I need my audience to laugh.
(hint)
But, and I think this is where I really am special, I very much resent them when they do.

Their smiles look like rictus grins.
I see the skulls behind the faces bulging.
I bring down the cleaver.
You've been a lovely audience.
If I was capable of love I'd love you all.
Laugh.
Applause.
And he does, he applauds along, he may even have whistled because he's American but he doesn't laugh.
He hasn't laughed once.

Everyone had a good set.
Everyone's feeling 'buzzed'.
Gavin had some telly people in.
The telly people saw me.
The telly people want to meet me.
You won't be able to open with the cum gag, Gavin says.
'That's what she said' which doesn't make much sense but the telly people laugh.

The American spends a lot of time talking to Djosephine and Ziggy.
He's not laughing at them but Ziggy is a comedy groupie so she's about as funny as that sounds so nothing to worry about there.
You were funny tonight, Gavin says. And then looking at the American: 'You bring nothing to the relationship.'
It's objectively a good night.

What's wrong?
I'm so depressed I have only just registered the fact that we're in his flat.
I've made it into the inner sanctum.
He lives in Hackney with a girl who is watching Netflix in the living room so we have to go into his bedroom.
I'm in his bedroom.
There is his bed.

What's wrong?
Nothing, I lie.
It was great. I had a great night. Your friends are great.
They're not my friends.
I mean the other comics.
I mean they are my friends we just don't like each other also we call them comedians. (I'm being a dick.) So…?
So…
What did you think?
You were hilarious.
Okay.
I don't know how you do it.
Do what?
Get up there.
I use my legs.
I mean I didn't get all the references but you know. Amazing.
Amazing.
He kisses me.
I hesitate.
What?
Nothing.
We kiss again.

Can I ask about the bloody cum?
Which is a fair enough question.
Doesn't happen any more, not a big deal, only lasted for three or four... months.
Wow. That must have been.
It's fine. It's all good copy.
Okay.
And he kisses me again but there's still the niggle. Why didn't the fucker laugh?
I didn't think the stuff about my dad really landed. (This is a lie, I'm just fishing, the stuff about my dad was gold.)
He looks at me.
Well it is sad.
Not really.
I mean you were making it into a joke but it was still kinda sad. You were so young.
I was twenty-one.
It was a trauma. Losing your dad at such a pivotal moment in your development, just when you're supposed to be coming into yourself you have to move home and look after your mum?
That is a trauma.
It was just a bit about oversized party sausages.

He shrugs: it just makes me sad to think about you being so alone.

That's what he says, just like that, like it's an easy thing to say:

'It just makes me sad to think about you being so alone.'

I have a feeling I've done something terribly wrong but I can't remember what.
I have a feeling I've been caught out in a massive lie.
I have a feeling any second now, someone is going to knock on the door and take me away.

Except.
Except that of course that's what I want him to feel.
I want him to feel sad for me.
I want him to sense the pain beneath the jokes, the dead bodies buried in a shallow grave of weird sex and passive-aggressive asides.

And I want you to sense it too, obviously.
But I don't want to talk about it.
If I wanted to talk about it I wouldn't layer it in irony, encase it in the meta, I wouldn't be making jokes now would I?
But you get that. We get that. We don't have to talk about it?
That would be boring; that wouldn't be funny.
But here, here he is talking about it.
Naming it.
Here he is and yes I'm going to say it.
Seeing me.

And I cry.
Okay.
Happy?

But honestly these are weird tears.
Very weird tears.
They come without trying.
(Without a conscious, constipated attempt to feel something.
Without even the aid of Bette Midler in *Beaches*.)
They're just there.
He kisses them which just makes me cry more.
And then I'm laughing like one of those people.
One of those people on the telly feeling things.
Stay here, he says. Stay with me.
And we're kissing and yes.
We're doing the sex but I manage to stay there.
I stay looking into his eyes as we remove each other's clothes.
I mean I do sneak the odd look, presumably he doesn't just want me to look into his eyes the whole –
He holds my face clamped in his hands fixed on his eyes.
(It was mental really but I went with it.)
And actually, actually, when it was just him and me.
When I wasn't distracted.
When I wasn't thinking.
I felt… things… which was…
Nice.
The sex was nice.

Now nice of course is a loaded word.
And I don't mean to say that it was boring.

I just mean I didn't feel shit after.
Which in that moment, I realised, might have been a first.
Which makes me cry.
Again.
And he is adorable.
He holds me in the arms and yes, I can't help but notice the arms are the arms of a Disney prince.
And he whispers things, I forget what now and they were probably cheesy but he wasn't afraid to say them.
If it was me in that situation I would already be offering tea and asking if he wanted to be on his own.
Because I'm awful. I'm the worst.
You're beautiful he says.
And I say what's wrong with you?
What do you mean?
You're just perfect? You're perfect aren't you? What's wrong with you?

I've stopped crying by now, just you know, for context and he's moved away.
He's standing in the middle of the room naked.
I don't know how people do that.
Just stand there naked in front of someone else but he does it.
He stands there, naked, looking to all intents and purposes like the guy Michelangelo dumped David for when he got rich and famous and he says – I have to tell you something.
Which of course we know is the end.
Perhaps not the end-end but the beginning of the end.
A state of calm descends on me.
I'm completely serene.
I'm swimming in Lake Me.
It's more like a pond and I've clearly shat in it but it's mine.
Here it comes.

I can't laugh.

What?

I can't laugh. If I laugh I could die.

What do you mean?

It's a nerve condition.

Are you serious?

Deadly. He says, and almost but doesn't actually laugh.

He can't.

/

Ever hear the one about the comedian with the boyfriend who can't laugh?

/

And it's true.
It is true.
It is a genuine medical condition.
It's called cataplexy.
It's a bit like narcolepsy which I've always had a fondness for ever since *My Own Private Idaho*.
River Phoenix repeatedly swooning in Keanu Reeves' arms was actually something of a sexual awakening for me.
Is it like that?
He hadn't seen it, of course.
So…
So… If you laugh your head falls off?
Not exactly he says. But worst-case I could die.
Right.
Or there is a risk of permanent paralysis.
Right.
I just have to be careful.
Right.
I've sort of learnt to train myself to be on guard.
Right.
I can feel it coming, he says.
Now?
No. Not now.
I'm using humour to defuse the tension.
I know.
And that's bad?
No.
I just have to not be too funny.
Which shouldn't be a problem.

Which is funny.
Which is a joke so I laugh and then stop myself.
You can laugh, you're allowed to laugh, it's just me. I can't laugh.
Okay.
Is this going to be a problem? He asks.

/

Of course it's not a problem.
And, dear readers, wait for it... it isn't.

Imagine almost complete happiness.
No, me either but try.
We start seeing each other repeatedly, regularly in a way that starts to resemble, gasp,
people in a relationship.
I have no experience of this, I'm just basing it off *Friends*.
(My entire generation does and yes frankly that is a problem but let's pretend it isn't for a minute okay? Yes? No? Great.)
There are the galleries where suddenly we are in complete agreement about every painting,
trips to the cinema to see obscure foreign-language films
I finally seem able to enjoy, documentary nights in his bedroom.
Actually he's very into documentaries, the more hard-hitting the better.
What with the head-falling-off situation we spend a lot of time snuggling down to the latest doc about the Cambodian killing fields and smiling.
At each other.
Not the.
I meet a couple of his friends, once.
The flatmate knows my name.
I think she's called Charlotte.
Or Francesca.
One of the two.
Neither of us have ever seen her not watching Netflix in the living room.

The summer is long and endless-feeling.
I get a bike, immediately realise I've forgotten how to ride a bike; turns out it's not at all like riding a bike.

It's actually really hard.
I'm wobbly but strangely fearless as long as I'm with him.
We cycle to Essex which, who knew? is basically in the country and actually quite nice.
The American is an excellent cook so I put on weight but in interesting places.
My body is changing, I'm filling out.
Like someone has drawn my outline in ink, finally.
I'm me but a new me.
A grown-up me.
And that in itself feels exciting.
And the porousness of long summer days into long summer nights and the him and the me grows until there's no need to clarify whether we *are* seeing each other because we *only* see each other.

He doesn't come to my gigs.
I don't need him to.
I mean I don't go to his lectures do I?
The demand for affirmation seems suddenly insane.
What on earth am I doing, talking into people's faces demanding their laughter, demanding their love?
Because it's not love is it?
What I have with the American.
That…

Beat.

I experiment with my material.
Tone down the trauma and the bloody cum.
I start talking about how different but compatible me and the American are.
Stuff about British versus American sensibilities.
He's always the hero, and I'm still the idiot but you know, a more likeable idiot.
More Hugh Grant less Philip Roth.

Djosephine doesn't like the new material but she's in a bad mood.
She recently broke up with her girlfriend, Ziggy.
Apparently Ziggy recited the whole of the Dead Parrot Sketch during sex one night and Djospehine snapped.
Ruined the vibe? I asked.

Ruined the sketch. She has terrible timing.
We agree that's a good line and she should use it.

Gavin's into my new set which may or may not be a worry.
I have a screen test for a new panel show coming up.
Life is good.
I text Michael, the doctor.

Just you know, 'how are you?'
He responds
'What's up?'
And what's up is my penis, immediately just like that.
I take a moment.
I breathe.
(I'm breathing now. The American has got me into something called breath work. Turns out I've been breathing wrong my entire life which I fully believe.)
So, I breathe and say:
'Hey, dude.' (I don't know why we do that.) 'Not much. I'm good though. I've got a boyf exclamation mark.'
And then press send.
Immediate relief.
He writes back immediately in flowing prose I didn't know he was capable of about how happy he was for me, how lucky the guy is and on and on and how we should get tea some time.
Tea?
I think about not responding but that would be rude, that would be game-playing and there's no need to game-play because we're just friends.
Thanks. Tea would be lovely. Actually. I'm doing a stand-up in Kilburn tomorrow. Not too far from you question mark. Want to come question mark.'
He doesn't respond.
Which is fine.
Which is good.

The next night in Kilburn, I look for him in the audience.
There's a feeling.
What is that feeling?
I feel shit about myself that's it.

I channel it into the comedy.
I phase out the American and become comedically, tragically single again.
I get more laughs.

/

Have you ever stroked a kitten and thought?: 'my hand is bigger than its head and if I just…'

/

Michael texts about missing the Kilburn show.
Twenty-three days after the Kilburn show.
No worries, I reply instantly. How are you?
Good he texts, and then sends through a picture of a naked guy puckered out on his bed.
'Hahaha. Is this happening live?' I write.
He responds, it is.
I don't respond
I shouldn't respond.
I send a winky face.
He sends one back.
When I find myself wanking to the message exchange later, it's not because of the picture Michael sent but of the almost painfully exquisite eroticism of our two winking emojis.
One on top of the other.

/

The American doesn't get slapstick.
This isn't surprising but I'm acting surprised.

It's absolutely pure comedy, I explain.
I don't find it funny.
That's not possible. It's instinctively funny.
To see someone getting hurt?
No, it's really important they don't get hurt. That's the difference between comedy and tragedy. What's funny, I pontificate, is the complete upturning of reality in one moment. I'm in a pub, I'm drinking a pint, I'm leaning back towards the bar because that's where the bar is but it's not and I fall through.
I don't get it.

I think it's about death.
You think everything is about death.
No, listen. We see someone fall over and get hurt. That's not funny. We see someone lean against a bar but there's no bar there, he falls through and then gets up that's funny. Something weird has happened, something out of the ordinary has happened but no one is hurt.
How is that about death?
One of these days we're going to fall and we're not going to get up but not this time. In that moment of resurrection we realise how alive we are and the relief is the laughter.
It all just seems silly to me.
Okay, what do you find funny?
You know what I find funny.
Werner Herzog documentaries?
Shut up. You, I find you funny.
Lies.
I find lots of things funny.
Name them.
Like people, comedians?
Or whatever.
Bill Hicks.
Doesn't count.
Why doesn't that count?
Because I love Bill Hicks, everyone loves Bill Hicks but no one actually laughs out loud at Bill Hicks. What makes you laugh?
Why? Why do you need to know what makes me laugh?
And it's a good question.

/

The therapist looks at me for the first time.
She's not a real therapist.
I can't afford that.
She's a nice girl from the NHS with no detectable shoulders.
What I do and what we can offer is something called CBT, which stands for Cognitive Behavioural Therapy.
I just need to talk to someone.
Also you do know that in some circles, CBT stands for Cock and Ball Torture?
(She shifts in her seat.)

Thank you for filling in the questionnaires.
No problem.
I can see for the section where we ask you to grade on a scale a feeling that something terrible is going to happen you have put ten out of the maximum ten?
Yes.
And for the question about whether you might be at risk of hurting others, you've put ten out of ten, written YES and underlined it three times.
Yes, that's what I wanted to talk about.
Can I ask why you've also drawn a smiley face?
Well, I also want you to like me.

(She makes a note in her pad for the first time, which I'm excited about.)

Can you outline the nature of the risk you pose?
Have you ever stroked a kitten and thought 'my hand is bigger than its head and if I just...'
So you want to kill a kitten?
No, I want to make my boyfriend laugh.
(She looks confused.)
Which will kill him. It's a medical thing, if he laughs his head falls off.
My therapist laughs and stops herself.
Actually, I'm doing a show in Putney next week if... No, see this is the problem. I need an audience to laugh. I need you to laugh. I especially need him to laugh.
Why?
I don't know I just do.
Pause.
Maybe because I have feelings for him?
She nods encouragingly.
Would you say you have negative thought patterns?
I would say so, yes.
Do you have a tendency to catastrophise?
Every second of every day but that's not the point. What I want to know is am I a psychopath?
So what I do and what we can offer is something called CBT, which stands for Cognitive Behavioural Therapy.

Sorry.
Sorry.
I'll try again.

Ever since I texted Michael.
Ever since I invited him to the gig.
Ever since then things have been different.

I start feeling self-conscious around the American.
The calm, the intellectual nights out, even the nice sex.
The calm, perfect sex feels like a test.

I'm struggling to have normal conversations, instead I do bits at him, into his face.
I turn everything into a routine.
I catch myself sometimes and I say sorry, sorry.
Stop saying sorry, it's fine.
I think about tickling him.
His mouth fully open and the laugh.
The laugh?
What would that sound like?
I think out of the buff American would come the cutest little giggle.
And he is a bit camp, which I love.
I love him, I think.
He's so fucking nice I want his head to fall off.

And the thing is, no one would be able to prove anything – he has a condition.
It's the perfect crime.
But I'd confess.
I'd have to.
The hardest thing wouldn't be jail.
It would be facing his family.
And mine.
My mum's face as the jury says guilty.
Because I am.

Shall we watch *Nazi Megastructures* on Netflix?
Perfect I say.
And breathe shallowly.

I'm losing weight again.
Losing definition.

/

Michael texts again.
I don't respond though.
I don't respond.
I don't think.

A drug dealer on the way to Michael's asks if I want coke and I say yes, which comes as a surprise but appears to be true.
I mean it's going to be *awful*.

You can see Hampstead Heath from Michael's living room. We're sat on his sofa. Being friends.

You're getting skinny he says.

He shifts so we're facing each other: You look good skinny. Healthy skinny.

I look away.

He moves his knee so it touches mine.

I stay very still but I don't move away.

Have you heard of cataplexy?

No, well, sort of. Is that the laughing thing? Is that the latest thing you've got?

Stop making me out to be a hypochondriac.

You are a hypochondriac.

Yes but that doesn't mean I'm not ill. Or won't be. I mean if there's one thing in life that's guaranteed.

Have you ever actually seen anyone die? He asks.

No.

And it's true.
I never saw Dad die.
He died in hospital and I didn't make it in time.
I can't even be sure I saw his body before the funeral.

All I remember is my mum crying.
Crying is not the right word.

Talk to me after you have, he says.

Sorry, I say.

It's fine.

He leans forward for the kiss.

Oh so this is it?
This is a choice.

I kiss Michael.

I feel okay.
I don't feel stressed.
I don't feel guilty.
It's weird how fine I feel.
I actually feel suddenly powerful.
I know how to do this.
I suggest we get another guy around.

Beat.

Are you sure? Michael asks and I say… yeah why not?

We hang on opposite ends of his bed looking at The App, occasionally showing each other blurry pictures of strangers' cocks and snorting coke.

This one?
He holds up his phone to reveal a guy's face.
Unremarkable, inoffensive, funny lighting but beggars can't be choosers.

Him.

He takes ages to arrive.
The lighting was indeed funny and the picture was old.
He takes off his top self-consciously and asks who wants to get fucked.
We look at each other unsure.
Michael looks away, and even though I don't want to, seeing as it was my idea I say 'me, please'.

His dick is an odd fit and he puts on a voice to say things like:
dirty slut, dirty whore, going to fill you up.
I make sure the condom is in place and make noises.
Michael doesn't make eye contact.
I lie back and close my eyes.

I immediately see the American's smiling face exploding
against the back of my eyelids.
I open them.
The Random is still going at it.
I look around.
I can't see Michael.
He's gone.
I look back to see the Random has a camera.
Hey! Stop it.
I turn my face away.
Stop filming
You look hot.
Stop it.
I bury my face in the mattress.
Oh well, I think.
He keeps going.
I wait for it to stop.
After a while he cums.

I wait until I hear him get dressed.
And leave before I move.

Michael is on his sofa.

I sit beside him.
He gives me a lopsided grin.

Did you have fun? He asks.

What do you mean?

I snuggle into him.

He doesn't quite give.

In fact, he pulls away.

And then five four three two one.

Actually do you mind going home? I've got an early start.

And I say... of course, of course, no worries, obviously, cool, great, wicked (?), and as I'm leaving: cheers. Mate...

I catch him letting out a sigh of relief as the door closes fast behind me.

I go home.

The American has texted. Of course he has.

I should tell him.

I should tell him everything.

Explain everything. He'd understand.

He always understands everything, before I do, even.

He's so good.

Too good.

I don't text.

/

I don't text.

I just show up at the American's flat.
That's better.
It's midnight.
I don't ask.
I don't text.
I just show up at the American's flat.
Like they do in movies.
Like they do in *Friends* except I can still feel the lube in my hole and actually, actually, it turns out to be quite awkward because he's not in.
Charlotte slash Francesca is though and she lets me inside.
She's actually quite nice, we watch Netflix for a bit and then I go into his bedroom.
It's surprisingly messy, the remains of his breakfast by his bed, a cereal bowl, a banana peel.
Something about the spoon in the bowl and the bits of oats stuck to the bowl makes him feel real and I start crying.

I hear his voice outside.
He opens the door.
I stay seated, and cling to the edge of his bed, very aware all of a sudden that I'm still quite high.
Hello you. What's up?
I'm sorry.
Why?
I fucked up.
What happened?
And I tell him.
I tell him about the jogger.
He doesn't give much away.
I tell him about Michael.
About our texts.
About the threesome no one wanted.
And how I'd had enough.
And how all I really wanted was him.

He stands up.
Zach, I say.
His name is Zach.
Or Joey? Ross? Pacey? Dawson? It doesn't really matter.
You are so interesting and clever and you've introduced me to so many great World War II documentaries.
Don't do that.
Sorry. I'll start again. (*Pause*.) I fuck up. I keep fucking up, but I don't want to, I don't want to any more. I just do it because it's easier. Which makes no sense I know but this feels rare and special but really, really fragile and I'm really scared. I know that's not enough and every bit of me wants to do a bit right now and maybe I am right now, fuck me. But I'm trying, I'm trying not to. I'm trying to say. You know what I'm trying to say.
I don't. I honestly don't.
I'm trying to say…
Well?
What?
Say it then.
What do you mean?

Say the words.
And?
And…
I.
I.
I.
Can't.
Okay, he says and turns away.
(*Quickly.*) I love you.
It's the first time I've said it aloud ever.
I hope it's enough.
It doesn't feel enough.
(*Louder.*) I love you.
(*Softer.*) I love you.
He is very quiet.
Very quiet.

It's not working.
It's supposed to work.
It always works on TV.

I stand up too quickly to reach out to him and bash my head against a dangling lampshade which wasn't there a minute ago.
I step back into the cereal bowl, try and steady myself but my other foot finds the banana peel, I slip.
And I fall flat on my back.
Splat.

Beat.

I hear a sound I don't recognise at first.
A giggle.
Then a laugh.
A camp-as-tits laugh.
I see him standing above me, laughing with those teeth.
A pop of his pretty pink tongue.
White teeth, pink tongue.
And then he's gone.
And the laughing stops.
I hear a gurgling.
I pull myself up.

I see his legs sticking out from behind the other side of the bed.
I run towards the legs.
His body doesn't seem right.
The angles are strange but his eyes are still open.
I call out his name.
The eyes stop.
His eyes just stop.
And I'm not supposed to say this but there is a little part of me that is glad.
There is a little part that thinks I could never have made it work.
There is a little part of me that wonders if he was always too good to be true.
And then I hear his breathing stop and everything in me falls apart.

He cries.

And then.
And then.
And then just like that…
He winks.
The little fucker smiles… and winks.

Beat.

(*Quietly.*) Thank you. You've been a lovely audience.

Blackout.

End.

A Nick Hern Book

Feeling Afraid As If Something Terrible Is Going To Happen first published in Great Britain in 2022 as a paperback original by Nick Hern Books Limited, The Glasshouse, 49a Goldhawk Road, London W12 8QP, in association with Francesca Moody Productions

Reprinted with revisions in 2023

Feeling Afraid As If Something Terrible Is Going To Happen copyright © 2022, 2023 Marcelo Dos Santos

Marcelo Dos Santos has asserted his right to be identified as the author of this work

Cover image: Photography by The Other Richard; cover design by Thread

Designed and typeset by Nick Hern Books, London

Printed in Great Britain by Mimeo Ltd, Huntingdon, Cambridgeshire PE29 6XX

A CIP catalogue record for this book is available from the British Library

ISBN 978 1 83904 259 1

CAUTION All rights whatsoever in this play are strictly reserved. Requests to reproduce the text in whole or in part should be addressed to the publisher.

Amateur Performing Rights Applications for performance, including readings and excerpts, by amateurs in English should be addressed to the Performing Rights Manager, Nick Hern Books, The Glasshouse, 49a Goldhawk Road, London W12 8QP, *tel* +44 (0)20 8749 4953, *email* rights@nickhernbooks.co.uk, except as follows:

Australia: ORiGiN Theatrical, *email* enquiries@originmusic.com.au, *web* www.origintheatrical.com.au

New Zealand: Play Bureau, 20 Rua Street, Mangapapa, Gisborne, 4010, *tel* +64 21 258 3998, *email* info@playbureau.com

United States of America and Canada: The Agency (London) Ltd, see details below

Professional Performing Rights Applications for performance by professionals in any medium and in any language throughout the world (and amateur and stock performances in the United States of America and Canada) should be addressed to The Agency (London) Ltd, 24 Pottery Lane, Holland Park, London W11 4LZ, *fax* +44 (0)20 7727 9037, *email* info@theagency.co.uk

No performance of any kind may be given unless a licence has been obtained. Applications should be made before rehearsals begin. Publication of this play does not necessarily indicate its availability for amateur performance.

www.nickhernbooks.co.uk

facebook.com/nickhernbooks

twitter.com/nickhernbooks